Cozy Christmas Cookies & Sweet Treats

Introduction

Imagine your kitchen filled with the warm scent of cinnamon and vanilla, the soft glow of Christmas lights twinkling as you pull a tray of perfect cookies from the oven. For beginner cooks and Christmas enthusiasts, the holiday season can feel overwhelming—complex recipes, endless ingredient lists, and the fear of disappointing loved ones with lackluster treats. Cozy Christmas Cookies & Sweet Treats - Advent Calendar Cookbook is your festive solution, designed to make baking simple, joyful, and oh-so-delicious.

This cookbook unfolds like an advent calendar, with 24 doors—one for each day leading up to Christmas. Behind each door, you'll find two beginner-friendly recipes for cookies and sweet treats, totaling 48 festive creations. From white chocolate cranberry cookies to fudge snowballs, every recipe is crafted for ease and holiday cheer, helping you build confidence and create memories without stress.

Here's what you'll love:

- ***Daily Delight:*** *Two new recipes each day to keep the holiday spirit alive.*
- ***Simple Steps:*** *Clear, foolproof instructions for beginners.*
- ***Festive Magic:*** *Recipes bursting with Christmas flavors to impress guests.*
- ***Joyful Moments:*** *Create traditions that warm hearts and homes.*

Picture your family savoring your treats, their smiles lighting up your holiday gatherings. No more fear of failure—just the joy of baking. Start on December 1st, open the first door, and let the magic begin!

Bonus cooking video:

In addition to this book, I have recorded a cooking video featuring my personal favorite Christmas sweets. Scan the QR code now, enter your email address, and I will send you the video by email. I really hope you enjoy it!

Door 1

Soft Sugar Cookies

Total Time: 1 hour

These soft, chewy cookies melt in your mouth with delicate hints of cinnamon and spicy star anise. Their shimmering sugar exterior will remind you of the first snowflakes of winter.

- 2¾ cups all-purpose flour
- 1 tsp baking soda
- ½ tsp baking powder
- 1 cup unsalted butter, softened
- 1½ cups granulated sugar
- 1 large egg
- 1 tsp vanilla extract
- ½ tsp almond extract
- 3–4 tbsp milk
- ¾ cup granulated sugar (for coating)
- 1 tsp ground cinnamon (for coating)
- ¼ tsp ground star anise (for coating)

1. Preheat oven to 375°F (190°C) and line two baking sheets with parchment paper.
2. In a bowl, whisk flour, baking soda, and baking powder. In another bowl, beat butter and 1½ cups sugar until fluffy.
3. Add egg, vanilla, and almond extract. Mix well.
4. Gradually add dry ingredients. If the dough is dry, add 1 tbsp milk at a time until soft but not sticky.
5. Roll dough into 1-inch balls. Whisk ¾ cup sugar, cinnamon, and star anise in a small bowl. Roll each dough ball in the mixture to coat.
6. Place 2 inches apart on the baking sheets and flatten slightly.
7. Bake for 8–10 minutes. Cool on the sheet for 2 minutes, then transfer to a wire rack.

Vanilla Fudge Snowballs

Total Time: 20 minutes + 1 hour chilling

Creamy fudge bites with sweet vanilla are rolled in shredded coconut for a snowy welcome.

14 oz sweetened condensed milk
3 cups white chocolate chips
1 tsp vanilla extract
¼ tsp salt
1 cup shredded coconut (for coating)

1. Line an 8x8-inch baking dish with parchment paper, leaving overhang for easy removal.
2. In a medium saucepan over low heat, combine condensed milk and white chocolate chips. Stir constantly until melted and smooth (about 5 minutes).
3. Remove from heat and stir in vanilla extract and salt.
4. Pour the mixture into the prepared dish and smooth the top with a spatula.
5. Refrigerate for 1 hour, or until firm.
6. Remove fudge from the dish using the parchment overhang. Cut into 1-inch squares.
7. Roll each square into a ball and coat with shredded coconut to resemble snowballs. Store in an airtight container in the fridge.

Door 2

Soft Gingerbread Cookies

Total Time: 45 minutes

Chewy cookies burst with ginger and molasses, their sugary crunch feeling like a warm night by the fire.

- 3 cups all-purpose flour
- 1 tsp baking soda
- ¾ tsp ground cinnamon
- ¾ tsp ground ginger
- ½ tsp ground allspice
- ½ tsp ground cloves
- ½ tsp salt
- ¾ cup unsalted butter, softened
- ¾ cup dark brown sugar
- ½ cup molasses
- 1 large egg
- 1 tsp vanilla extract
- ½ cup granulated sugar (for rolling)

1. Preheat oven to 350°F (175°C). Line two baking sheets with parchment paper.
2. In a medium bowl, whisk together flour, baking soda, cinnamon, ginger, allspice, cloves, and salt. Set aside.
3. In a large bowl, beat butter and brown sugar with an electric mixer until creamy (about 2 minutes).
4. Add molasses, egg, and vanilla extract, beating until smooth.
5. Gradually add dry ingredients to the wet ingredients, mixing until a soft dough forms.
6. Roll dough into 1-inch balls, then roll each ball in granulated sugar to coat.
7. Place balls 2 inches apart on the prepared baking sheets. Bake for 10–12 minutes, until cookies are set but still soft in the center.
8. Let them cool on the baking sheets for 5 minutes, then transfer to a wire rack to cool completely.

Ginger Molasses Truffles

Total Time: 30 minutes + 2 hours chilling

Smooth dark chocolate hides a creamy ginger-molasses kick inside, perfect for cozying up fireside with a sweet treat.

- 2 cups gingersnap cookie crumbs (about 20 cookies)
- 8 oz cream cheese, softened
- ¼ cup molasses
- 1 tsp ground ginger
- ½ tsp ground cinnamon
- ¼ tsp ground cloves
- 12 oz dark chocolate chips
- 4 oz white chocolate chips (for decoration)

1. In a food processor, pulse gingersnap cookies into fine crumbs. Measure out 2 cups.
2. In a large bowl, beat cream cheese with an electric mixer until smooth. Add gingersnap crumbs, molasses, ginger, cinnamon, and cloves. Mix until well combined.
3. Roll mixture into 1-inch balls and place on a parchment-lined baking sheet. Freeze for 1 hour.
4. Melt dark chocolate chips in a microwave-safe bowl in 30-second intervals, stirring until smooth.
5. Dip each ball in melted chocolate using a fork, tapping off excess. Place back on parchment. Let set.
6. Melt white chocolate chips in a microwave-safe bowl in 30-second intervals, stirring until smooth. Drizzle over truffles. Refrigerate for 1 hour or until set.

Door 3

Cranberry Orange Shortbread Cookies

Total Time: 1 hour

Buttery shortbread pops with tart cranberry and zesty orange, like a fresh-picked winter orchard treat.

- 1 cup unsalted butter, softened
- ¾ cup powdered sugar
- 1 tsp vanilla extract
- 1 tbsp orange zest (from 1 orange)
- 2 cups all-purpose flour
- ¼ tsp salt
- ½ cup dried cranberries, finely chopped
- 2 tbsp granulated sugar (for sprinkling)

1. Preheat oven to 325°F (165°C). Line two baking sheets with parchment paper.
2. In a large bowl, cream butter and powdered sugar with an electric mixer until light and fluffy (about 2 minutes).
3. Add vanilla extract and orange zest, mixing until combined.
4. In a separate bowl, whisk together flour and salt. Gradually add to the butter mixture, mixing until just combined.
5. Fold in chopped cranberries with a spatula until evenly distributed.
6. Divide the dough in half. Roll each half into a log (about 1½ inches in diameter). Wrap in plastic wrap and refrigerate for 30 minutes.
7. Slice logs into ¼-inch thick rounds and place them 2 inches apart on the prepared baking sheets. Sprinkle lightly with granulated sugar.
8. Bake for 12–15 minutes, until edges are lightly golden. Cool on the baking sheets for 5 minutes, then transfer to a wire rack.

Apple Cranberry Fudge

Total Time: 25 minutes + 2 hours chilling

Creamy fudge blends sweet apples and tart cranberries, tasting like a snowy orchard walk in every bite.

- 3 cups white chocolate chips
- 14 oz sweetened condensed milk
- 1 tsp vanilla extract
- ¼ tsp ground cinnamon
- ½ cup dried cranberries
- ¼ cup dried apples, finely chopped
- Pinch of salt

1. Line an 8x8-inch baking dish with parchment paper, leaving overhang for easy removal.
2. In a medium saucepan over low heat, combine white chocolate chips and condensed milk. Stir constantly until melted and smooth (about 5–7 minutes).
3. Remove from heat and stir in vanilla extract, cinnamon, and salt.
4. Fold in cranberries and dried apples until evenly distributed.
5. Pour the mixture into the prepared dish and smooth the top with a spatula.
6. Refrigerate for 2 hours, or until firm.
7. Lift fudge from the baking dish using parchment overhang. Cut into 1-inch squares. Store in an airtight container in the fridge.

Door 4

Chocolate Peppermint Crinkle Cookies

Total Time: 45 minutes

Fudgy chocolate cookies have a cool peppermint zing, with powdered sugar that looks like a starry night.

1 cup all-purpose flour
½ cup unsweetened cocoa powder
1 tsp baking powder
¼ tsp salt
¾ cup granulated sugar
¼ cup vegetable oil
2 large eggs
1 tsp vanilla extract
½ tsp peppermint extract
½ cup powdered sugar (for rolling)

1. Preheat oven to 350°F (175°C). Line two baking sheets with parchment paper.
2. In a medium bowl, whisk together flour, cocoa powder, baking powder, and salt. Set aside.
3. In a large bowl, whisk granulated sugar and vegetable oil until combined. Add eggs, vanilla extract, and peppermint extract, whisking until smooth.
4. Gradually add dry ingredients to the wet ingredients, stirring until a soft dough forms.
5. Refrigerate dough for 15 minutes to make it easier to handle.
6. Scoop 1 tbsp of dough and roll into a ball. Roll each ball in powdered sugar to coat generously.
7. Place balls 2 inches apart on the baking sheets. Bake for 10–12 minutes, until cookies crackle on top.
8. Let them cool on the baking sheets for 5 minutes, then transfer to a wire rack to cool completely.

Peppermint Mocha Truffles

Total Time: 30 minutes + 1 hour chilling

Rich chocolate truffles with a coffee-peppermint kick that tastes like stars twinkling on a cold winter night.

- 8 oz semi-sweet chocolate chips
- ½ cup heavy cream
- 1 tsp instant coffee granules
- ½ tsp peppermint extract
- ¼ tsp vanilla extract
- ¼ cup cocoa powder (for coating)

1. Place chocolate chips in a heatproof bowl.
2. In a small saucepan, heat heavy cream over medium heat until just simmering (do not boil). Remove from heat and stir in coffee granules until dissolved.
3. Pour hot cream over chocolate chips. Let sit for 2 minutes, then stir until smooth.
4. Stir in peppermint extract and vanilla extract. Let mixture cool to room temperature (about 15 minutes).
5. Refrigerate for 1 hour, or until firm enough to scoop.
6. Scoop 1 tsp of mixture and roll into a ball. Repeat with remaining mixture.
7. Roll the truffles in cocoa powder. Store in an airtight container in the fridge.

Door 5

Cinnamon Spice Snickerdoodles

Total Time: 40 minutes

Soft, cinnamon-sugar dusted cookies with a hint of nutmeg taste like warm treats from a Christmas market stall.

- 2¾ cups all-purpose flour
- 2 tsp cream of tartar
- 1 tsp baking soda
- ½ tsp salt
- 1 tsp ground cinnamon
- ¼ tsp ground nutmeg
- 1 cup unsalted butter, softened
- 1½ cups granulated sugar
- 2 large eggs
- 1 tsp vanilla extract
- ¼ cup granulated sugar (for rolling)
- 1 tbsp ground cinnamon (for rolling)

1. Preheat oven to 400°F (200°C). Line two baking sheets with parchment paper.
2. In a medium bowl, whisk together flour, cream of tartar, baking soda, salt, cinnamon, and nutmeg. Set aside.
3. In a large bowl, cream butter and 1½ cups sugar with an electric mixer until light and fluffy (about 2 minutes).
4. Add eggs and vanilla extract, beating until combined.
5. Gradually add dry ingredients to the wet ingredients, mixing until a soft dough forms.
6. In a small bowl, mix ¼ cup sugar and 1 tbsp cinnamon for rolling.
7. Roll dough into 1-inch balls, then roll each ball in the cinnamon-sugar mixture to coat.
8. Place balls 2 inches apart on the baking sheets. Bake for 8–10 minutes, until edges are set and centers are soft.
9. Let them cool on the baking sheets for 5 minutes, then transfer to a wire rack to cool completely.

Nutmeg-Spiced Pralines

Total Time: 25 minutes + 1 hour cooling

These crunchy pecans with a sweet, nutmeg-spiced caramel snap like the best goodies you'd grab at a holiday market.

- 1½ cups granulated sugar
- ¾ cup light brown sugar, packed
- ½ cup heavy cream
- 6 tbsp unsalted butter
- ½ tsp ground nutmeg
- ¼ tsp salt
- 1½ cups whole pecans
- 1 tsp vanilla extract

1. Line a baking sheet with parchment paper and set aside.
2. In a medium saucepan, combine granulated sugar, brown sugar, heavy cream, butter, nutmeg, and salt. Cook over medium heat, stirring constantly, until mixture reaches a boil.
3. Stop stirring and let it boil for 3 minutes, or until a candy thermometer reads 235°F.
4. Remove from heat and stir in pecans and vanilla extract. Continue stirring for 1–2 minutes, until the mixture thickens slightly and becomes glossy.
5. Drop tablespoonfuls of mixture onto the prepared baking sheet, spacing them 2 inches apart.
6. Let pralines cool at room temperature for 1 hour, or until firm. Store in an airtight container.

Door 6

Snowman Oreo-Pops

Total Time: 35 minutes

These no-bake snowman Oreo-pops are the easiest and cutest sweet treats you'll make this holiday season.

- 12 Oreo cookies
- 1 cup white chocolate chips
- 12 lollipop sticks
- 24 small black candy eyes
- 12 small orange candy dots (for noses)
- 24 small black candy dots (for mouth)
- 1 tsp coconut oil (optional, for smoother chocolate)

1. Insert a lollipop stick into the cream filling of each Oreo cookie. Set aside.
2. Melt white chocolate chips with coconut oil in a microwave-safe bowl. Heat in 20-second intervals. Stir until smooth.
3. Dip each Oreo pop into the melted white chocolate. Coat completely to resemble snow.
4. Place pops on a parchment-lined tray. Let excess chocolate drip off.
5. Decorate each pop with 2 black candy eyes, 1 orange candy dot for a nose, and 5-6 black candy dots for a smiling mouth.
6. Chill in the refrigerator for 15-20 minutes until chocolate sets.

Peanut Butter Chocolate Fudge

Total Time: 20 minutes + 2 hours chilling

Velvety fudge mixes peanut butter and semi-sweet chocolate for a sweet treat Santa's reindeer will gladly enjoy.

1½ cups creamy peanut butter
1 cup semi-sweet chocolate chips
14 oz sweetened condensed milk
1 tsp vanilla extract
¼ tsp salt
¼ cup chopped peanuts (optional, for topping)

1. Line an 8x8-inch baking dish with parchment paper, leaving overhang for easy removal.
2. In a medium saucepan over low heat, combine peanut butter, chocolate chips, and sweetened condensed milk. Stir constantly until melted and smooth (about 5–7 minutes).
3. Remove from heat and stir in vanilla extract and salt.
4. Pour the mixture into the prepared dish and smooth the top with a spatula.
5. Sprinkle chopped peanuts, if using, evenly over the top, pressing lightly to adhere.
6. Refrigerate for 2 hours, or until firm.
7. Lift fudge from dish using parchment overhang. Cut into 1-inch squares. Store in an airtight container in the fridge.

Door 7

Almond Spritz Cookies

Total Time: 45 minutes

Light, buttery cookies with a nutty almond flavor and festive sanding sugar taste like a crisp winter day.

- 1 cup unsalted butter, softened
- ¾ cup granulated sugar
- 1 large egg
- 1 tsp almond extract
- 2¼ cups all-purpose flour
- ¼ tsp salt
- ¼ tsp baking powder
- 2 tbsp milk
- Red and green sanding sugar (for decoration)

1. Preheat oven to 375°F (190°C). Prepare a cookie press with desired shape (e.g., star, tree).
2. In a large bowl, cream butter and sugar with an electric mixer until light and fluffy (about 2 minutes).
3. Add egg and almond extract, beating until combined.
4. In a separate bowl, whisk together flour, salt, and baking powder.
5. Gradually add dry ingredients to wet ingredients, alternating with milk, mixing until a soft dough forms.
6. Fill cookie press with dough. Press cookies onto ungreased baking sheets, spacing 1 inch apart.
7. Sprinkle cookies with sanding sugar.
8. Bake for 8–10 minutes, until edges are lightly golden. Cool on sheets for 2 minutes, then transfer to a wire rack to cool completely.

Pecan Toffee Bites

Total Time: 30 minutes + 1 hour cooling

This crunchy toffee covered in chocolate snaps with nutty sweetness, like a frosty winter treat.

- ½ cup unsalted butter
- ¾ cup granulated sugar
- ¼ tsp salt
- 1 tsp vanilla extract
- 1 cup chopped pecans
- 1 cup semi-sweet chocolate chips

1. Line a 9x9-inch baking dish with parchment paper, leaving overhang for easy removal.
2. In a medium saucepan, melt butter over medium heat. Add sugar and salt, stirring constantly until sugar dissolves.
3. Bring mixture to a boil, stirring occasionally, until it reaches 300°F (hard-crack stage) on a candy thermometer (about 5–7 minutes).
4. Remove from heat and stir in vanilla extract.
5. Pour mixture into the prepared dish, spreading evenly with a spatula.
6. Sprinkle chocolate chips over the hot toffee. Let sit for 2 minutes, then spread melted chocolate evenly with a spatula. Sprinkle pecans on top.
7. Refrigerate for 1 hour, or until set. Break into bite-sized pieces. Store in an airtight container.

Door 8

Lemon Raspberry Thumbprint Cookies

Total Time: 50 minutes

Zesty lemon cookies hold tart raspberry jam, like holly berries bursting with flavor.

- 1 cup unsalted butter, softened
- ⅔ cup granulated sugar
- 1 tsp lemon zest (from 1 lemon)
- 1 tsp vanilla extract
- 2 cups all-purpose flour
- ¼ tsp salt
- ½ cup raspberry jam
- ½ cup powdered sugar
- 1–2 tsp lemon juice

1. Preheat oven to 350°F (175°C). Line two baking sheets with parchment paper.
2. In a large bowl, cream butter and granulated sugar with an electric mixer until light and fluffy (about 2 minutes).
3. Add lemon zest and vanilla extract, mixing until combined.
4. In a separate bowl, whisk together flour and salt. Gradually add to the butter mixture, mixing until a soft dough forms.
5. Roll dough into 1-inch balls and place 2 inches apart on baking sheets. Use your thumb to make an indentation in the center of each ball.
6. Fill each indentation with about ½ tsp raspberry jam.
7. Bake for 12–15 minutes, until edges are lightly golden. Cool on baking sheets for 5 minutes, then transfer to a wire rack.
8. For the glaze, whisk powdered sugar and lemon juice in a small bowl until smooth. Drizzle over cooled cookies.

Lemon Truffles

Total Time: 30 minutes + 2 hours chilling

Creamy white chocolate truffles pop with zesty lemon, their sugary coating shining like holly berries in the snow.

- 8 oz white chocolate chips
- ¼ cup heavy cream
- 2 tbsp lemon curd
- 1 tsp lemon zest (from 1 lemon)
- ½ tsp vanilla extract
- Yellow food coloring (optional)
- ¼ cup granulated sugar (for coating)
- 1 tbsp lemon zest (for coating)
- 1 tbsp shredded coconut (for coating)

1. Place white chocolate chips in a heatproof bowl.
2. In a small saucepan, heat heavy cream over medium heat until just simmering (do not boil). Remove from heat and stir in lemon curd, lemon zest, and vanilla extract. Add 1 drop of yellow food coloring, if using.
3. Pour hot cream mixture over white chocolate chips. Let sit for 2 minutes, then stir until smooth.
4. Refrigerate mixture for 2 hours, or until firm enough to scoop.
5. Scoop 1 tsp of mixture and roll into a ball. Repeat with the remaining mixture.
6. Mix the granulated sugar, lemon, zest, and shredded coconut in a small bowl. Roll each truffle in the mixture to coat. Store in an airtight container in the fridge.

Door 9

Brown Sugar Butterscotch Cookies

Total Time: 45 minutes

Chewy cookies with toasty butterscotch, milky white chocolate, and brown sugar. They taste like warm lights glowing in a snowy Christmas village.

- 2½ cups all-purpose flour
- 1 tsp baking soda
- ½ tsp salt
- ¾ cup unsalted butter, softened
- 1 cup light brown sugar, packed
- ½ cup granulated sugar
- 1 large egg
- 1 tsp vanilla extract
- ½ cup butterscotch chips
- ½ cup white chocolate chips

1. Preheat oven to 350°F (175°C). Line two baking sheets with parchment paper.
2. In a medium bowl, whisk together flour, baking soda, and salt. Set aside.
3. In a large bowl, cream butter, brown sugar, and granulated sugar with an electric mixer until light and fluffy (about 2 minutes).
4. Add egg and vanilla extract, beating until combined.
5. Gradually add dry ingredients to wet ingredients, mixing until just combined. Fold in butterscotch and white chocolate chips with a spatula.
6. Roll dough into 1-inch balls and place 2 inches apart on the baking sheets.
7. Bake for 10–12 minutes, until edges are golden but centers are soft. Cool on baking sheets for 5 minutes, then transfer to a wire rack to cool completely.

Butterscotch Fudge

Total Time: 25 minutes + 2 hours chilling

Smooth fudge with white chocolate, butterscotch, and crunchy walnuts tastes like a cozy treat from a winter cottage kitchen.

- 2 cups butterscotch chips
- 1 cup white chocolate chips
- 14 oz sweetened condensed milk
- 1 tsp vanilla extract
- ¼ tsp salt
- ¼ cup chopped walnuts (optional, for texture)

1. Line an 8x8-inch baking dish with parchment paper, leaving overhang for easy removal.
2. In a medium saucepan over low heat, combine butterscotch chips, white chocolate chips, and sweetened condensed milk. Stir constantly until melted and smooth (about 5–7 minutes).
3. Remove from heat and stir in vanilla extract, and salt.
4. Pour the mixture into the prepared dish and smooth the top with a spatula. Sprinkle with chopped walnuts, if using.
5. Refrigerate for 2 hours, or until firm.
6. Lift fudge from dish using parchment overhang. Cut into 1-inch squares. Store in an airtight container in the fridge.

Door 10

Austrian Linzer Cookies

Total Time: 1 hour

Buttery almond cookies with sweet raspberry jam taste like a warm hug from an Austrian alpine bakery.

- 1 cup unsalted butter, softened
- ¾ cup granulated sugar
- 1 large egg
- 1 tsp vanilla extract
- ½ tsp almond extract
- 2 cups all-purpose flour
- ¾ cup almond flour
- ½ tsp ground cinnamon
- ¼ tsp salt
- ½ cup raspberry jam
- ¼ cup powdered sugar (for dusting)

1. Preheat oven to 350°F (175°C). Line two baking sheets with parchment paper.
2. In a large bowl, cream butter and sugar with a mixer until light and fluffy (about 2 minutes).
3. Add egg, vanilla extract, and almond extract, beating until combined.
4. In a separate bowl, whisk flour, almond flour, cinnamon, and salt.
5. Gradually add dry ingredients to the wet ingredients, mixing until a dough forms.
6. Divide the dough in half, wrap in plastic wrap, and refrigerate for 30 minutes.
7. Roll out one portion of dough to ⅛-inch thickness on a floured surface. Cut out cookies with a 2-inch round cutter. Use a smaller cutter to cut out the center of half the cookies (for tops).
8. Place cookies 1-inch apart on baking sheets. Bake for 10–12 minutes. Cool on baking sheets for 5 minutes.
9. Spread ½ tsp raspberry jam on the bottom (whole) cookies. Place a cut-out cookie on top to create a sandwich. Dust with powdered sugar.

Raspberry Pecan Truffles

Total Time: 30 minutes + 2 hours chilling

These dark chocolate truffles with tart raspberry jam and nutty pecan crunch are like a sweet find in an alpine Christmas village.

8 oz dark chocolate chips
½ cup heavy cream
2 tbsp raspberry jam
½ tsp vanilla extract
¼ tsp salt
½ cup finely chopped pecans (for coating)

1. Place dark chocolate chips in a heatproof bowl.
2. In a small saucepan, heat heavy cream over medium heat until just simmering (do not boil). Remove from heat and stir in raspberry jam, vanilla extract, and salt.
3. Pour hot cream mixture over chocolate chips. Let sit for 2 minutes, then stir until smooth.
4. Refrigerate mixture for 2 hours, or until firm enough to scoop.
5. Scoop 1 tsp of mixture and roll into a ball. Repeat with the remaining mixture.
6. Roll each truffle in chopped pecans to coat. Store in an airtight container in the fridge.

11

Door 11

Coconut Snowball Truffles

Total Time: 20 minutes + 2 hours chilling

These rich, white chocolate truffles rolled in shredded coconut are easy, elegant bites for your Christmas celebrations.

- 12 oz white chocolate chips
- ½ cup heavy cream
- 2 tbsp unsalted butter
- 1 tsp vanilla extract
- 1 cup shredded coconut
- Pinch of salt
- Extra shredded coconut (for rolling)

1. Heat heavy cream and butter in a saucepan over medium heat. Stir until butter melts.
2. Pour hot cream mixture over white chocolate chips in a bowl. Let sit for 2 minutes.
3. Stir until chocolate is fully melted and smooth. Add vanilla extract and salt.
4. Chill mixture in the refrigerator for 2-3 hours until firm.
5. Scoop tablespoon-sized portions. Roll into balls with your hands.
6. Spread extra shredded coconut on a plate. Roll each truffle in coconut to coat.
7. Store in an airtight container in the fridge. Serve chilled.

Cranberry Pistachio White Chocolate Bark

Total Time: 15 minutes + 1 hour chilling

Crunchy white bark with green pistachios and red cranberries sparkles like Santa's favorite Christmas sleigh.

- 2 cups white chocolate chips
- ½ cup dried cranberries
- ½ cup pistachios, shelled and chopped
- ½ tsp ground cinnamon
- ¼ tsp ground nutmeg
- ¼ tsp ground ginger
- 1 tbsp coconut oil (optional, for smoother melting)
- Pinch of salt

1. Preheat oven to 350°F. Spread pistachios on a baking sheet.
2. Toast pistachios in the oven for 5-7 minutes until fragrant. Let cool and chop if not already done.
3. Melt white chocolate chips with coconut oil in a microwave-safe bowl. Heat in 20-second intervals.
4. Stir in cinnamon, nutmeg, ginger, and salt until evenly mixed.
5. Spread melted chocolate onto a parchment-lined baking sheet into a thin layer.
6. Sprinkle dried cranberries and chopped pistachios evenly over the chocolate.
7. Chill in the refrigerator for 1-2 hours until set. Break into pieces and serve.

12

Door 12

Espresso Chocolate Chip Cookies

Total Time: 40 minutes

Chewy cookies with espresso and chocolate chips warm you up like coffee on a calm December morning.

- 2¼ cups all-purpose flour
- 1 tsp baking soda
- ½ tsp salt
- 1 tbsp instant espresso powder
- ¾ cup unsalted butter, softened
- ¾ cup light brown sugar, packed
- ½ cup granulated sugar
- 1 large egg
- 1 tsp vanilla extract
- 1½ cups semi-sweet chocolate chips

1. Preheat oven to 375°F (190°C). Line two baking sheets with parchment paper.
2. In a medium bowl, whisk together flour, baking soda, salt, and espresso powder. Set aside.
3. In a large bowl, cream butter, brown sugar, and granulated sugar with an electric mixer until light and fluffy (about 2 minutes).
4. Add egg and vanilla extract, beating until combined.
5. Gradually add dry ingredients to wet ingredients, mixing until just combined. Fold in chocolate chips.
6. Scoop 1 tbsp of dough and roll into a ball. Place balls 2 inches apart on baking sheets.
7. Bake for 9–11 minutes, until edges are set but centers are soft. Cool on the baking sheets for 5 minutes, then transfer to a wire rack to cool completely.

Mocha Hazelnut Truffles

Total Time: 20 minutes + 2 hours chilling

Smooth mocha truffles with crunchy hazelnuts feel like a quiet, nutty treat under candlelit serenity.

- 12 oz dark chocolate chips (60-70% cocoa)
- ½ cup heavy cream
- 1 tbsp instant coffee granules
- 2 tbsp unsalted butter
- ½ cup hazelnuts, toasted and finely chopped
- ¼ cup unsweetened cocoa powder (for coating)
- Pinch of salt

1. Heat heavy cream and instant coffee granules in a saucepan over medium heat. Stir until coffee dissolves.
2. Pour hot cream mixture over dark chocolate chips in a bowl. Let sit for 2 minutes.
3. Stir until chocolate is fully melted and smooth. Add butter and salt. Mix well.
4. Fold in chopped hazelnuts. Chill mixture in the refrigerator for 2-3 hours until firm.
5. Scoop tablespoon-sized portions. Roll into balls or drops with your hands.
6. Place cocoa powder in a shallow dish. Roll each truffle in cocoa powder to coat. Refrigerate and serve chilled.

Door 13

Pistachio Mint Cookies

Total Time: 45 minutes

Crunchy pistachio cookies with cool mint taste like a walk through a snowy pine forest.

- 2 cups all-purpose flour
- ½ tsp baking powder
- ¼ tsp salt
- ¾ cup unsalted butter, softened
- ¾ cup granulated sugar
- 1 large egg
- 1 tsp vanilla extract
- ½ tsp mint extract
- ¾ cup shelled pistachios, finely chopped

1. Preheat oven to 350°F (175°C). Line two baking sheets with parchment paper.
2. In a medium bowl, whisk together flour, baking powder, and salt. Set aside.
3. In a large bowl, cream butter and sugar with an electric mixer until light and fluffy (about 2 minutes).
4. Add egg, vanilla extract, and mint extract, beating until combined.
5. Gradually add dry ingredients to the wet ingredients, mixing until a soft dough forms. Fold in chopped pistachios.
6. Roll dough into 1-inch balls and place 2 inches apart on the baking sheets. Flatten slightly with your hand.
7. Bake for 10–12 minutes, until edges are set. Cool on baking sheets for 5 minutes, then transfer to a wire rack to cool completely.

Mint Pistachio Fudge

Total Time: 25 minutes + 2 hours chilling

Creamy fudge with mint and pistachios melts like fresh snow on pine branches in a quiet forest.

2½ cups white chocolate chips
14 oz sweetened condensed milk
½ tsp mint extract
¼ tsp salt
1-2 drops green food coloring (optional)
1 cup shelled pistachios, roughly chopped

1. Line an 8x8-inch baking dish with parchment paper, leaving overhang for easy removal.
2. In a medium saucepan over low heat, combine white chocolate chips and sweetened condensed milk. Stir constantly until melted and smooth (about 5–7 minutes).
3. Remove from heat and stir in mint extract, salt, and green food coloring (if using).
4. Fold in ¾ cup pistachios until evenly distributed.
5. Pour the mixture into the prepared dish and smooth the top with a spatula.
6. Lightly press remaining ¼ cup pistachios on top. Refrigerate for 2 hours, or until firm.
7. Lift fudge from the baking dish using parchment overhang. Cut into 1-inch squares. Store in an airtight container in the fridge.

14

Door 14

Spiced Plum Jam Cookies

Total Time: 50 minutes

Soft cookies with tart plum jam and warm spices feel like sugar plums dancing in your mouth.

- 2 cups all-purpose flour
- ½ tsp baking powder
- ¼ tsp ground cinnamon
- ¼ tsp ground nutmeg
- ¼ tsp salt
- ¾ cup unsalted butter, softened
- ¾ cup granulated sugar
- 1 large egg
- 1 tsp vanilla extract
- ¼ cup plum jam

1. Preheat oven to 350°F (175°C). Line two baking sheets with parchment paper.
2. In a medium bowl, whisk together flour, baking powder, cinnamon, nutmeg, and salt. Set aside.
3. In a large bowl, cream butter and sugar with an electric mixer until light and fluffy (about 2 minutes).
4. Add egg and vanilla extract, beating until combined.
5. Gradually add dry ingredients to wet ingredients, mixing until a soft dough forms.
6. Roll dough into 1-inch balls and place 2 inches apart on baking sheets. Use your thumb to make an indentation in the center of each ball.
7. Fill each indentation with about ½ tsp plum jam.
8. Bake for 12–15 minutes, until edges are lightly golden. Cool on baking sheets for 5 minutes, then transfer to a wire rack.

Plum Spice Truffles

Total Time: 30 minutes + 2 hours chilling

Chocolate truffles with spiced plums melt sweetly, like a dreamy sugar plum from a Christmas ballet.

- 8 oz dark chocolate chips
- ½ cup heavy cream
- ¼ cup dried plums (prunes), finely chopped
- ½ tsp ground cinnamon
- ¼ tsp ground nutmeg
- ½ tsp vanilla extract
- ¼ tsp salt
- ¼ cup cocoa powder (for coating)

1. Place dark chocolate chips in a heatproof bowl.
2. In a small saucepan, heat heavy cream over medium heat until just simmering (do not boil). Remove from heat and stir in chopped dried plums, cinnamon, nutmeg, vanilla extract, and salt.
3. Pour hot cream mixture over chocolate chips. Let sit for 2 minutes, then stir until smooth.
4. Refrigerate mixture for 2 hours, or until firm enough to scoop.
5. Scoop 1 tsp of mixture and roll into a ball. Repeat with the remaining mixture.
6. Roll each truffle in cocoa powder to coat. Store in an airtight container in the fridge.

15

Door 15

Peppermint Chocolate Snowflake Cookies

Total Time: 50 minutes

Buttery cookies with dark chocolate and crushed candy canes taste like a sweet stroll on Candy Cane Lane.

- 2 ¾ cups all-purpose flour
- 1 cup unsalted butter, softened
- ¾ cup granulated sugar
- 1 large egg
- 1 tsp vanilla extract
- ½ tsp salt
- 8 oz dark chocolate chips (for dipping)
- ½ cup candy canes, crushed (for topping)
- 1 tsp baking powder

1. Preheat oven to 350°F. Line a baking sheet with parchment paper.
2. Cream butter and sugar in a bowl until light and fluffy. Add egg and vanilla extract.
3. Whisk flour, baking powder, and salt in another bowl. Gradually mix into the butter mixture.
4. Roll dough to ¼-inch thickness on a floured surface. Cut out snowflake shapes with a cookie cutter.
5. Place cookies on the baking sheet. Bake for 8-10 minutes until edges are lightly golden.
6. Melt dark chocolate chips in a microwave-safe bowl. Heat in 20-second intervals. Stir until smooth.
7. Dip half of each cooled cookie into melted chocolate. Sprinkle with crushed candy canes. Let set on parchment paper.

Peppermint Bark

Total Time: 20 minutes + 1 hour chilling

Semi-sweet and milky white chocolate layers crunch with peppermint, like candy canes lining a festive street.

12 oz semi-sweet chocolate chips
12 oz white chocolate chips
½ tsp peppermint extract
¾ cup crushed peppermint candies (about 12 candy canes)

1. Line a baking sheet with parchment paper.
2. In a microwave-safe bowl, melt semi-sweet chocolate chips in 30-second intervals, stirring until smooth. Spread onto the prepared baking sheet in a thin, even layer (about ¼-inch thick).
3. Refrigerate for 15 minutes, or until set.
4. In another microwave-safe bowl, melt white chocolate chips in 30-second intervals, stirring until smooth. Stir in peppermint extract.
5. Spread white chocolate over the set semi-sweet chocolate layer. Sprinkle crushed peppermint candies evenly over the top, pressing lightly to adhere.
6. Refrigerate for 45 minutes, or until fully set.
7. Break bark into bite-sized pieces. Store in an airtight container in the fridge.

Door 16

German Lebkuchen Cookies

Total Time: 50 minutes

Chewy cookies with spicy anise and toasty molasses glow like spiced treats from a German Christmas market.

- 2½ cups all-purpose flour
- ½ tsp baking soda
- ½ tsp ground cinnamon
- ½ tsp ground ginger
- ¼ tsp ground anise
- ¼ tsp ground cloves
- ¼ tsp salt
- ½ cup unsalted butter, softened
- ¾ cup dark brown sugar, packed
- ⅓ cup molasses
- 1 large egg
- 1 tsp vanilla extract
- 1 cup powdered sugar
- 2–3 tbsp lemon juice

1. Preheat oven to 350°F (175°C). Line two baking sheets with parchment paper.
2. In a medium bowl, whisk together flour, baking soda, cinnamon, ginger, anise, cloves, and salt. Set aside.
3. In a large bowl, cream butter and brown sugar with an electric mixer until light and fluffy (about 2 minutes).
4. Add molasses, egg, and vanilla extract, beating until combined.
5. Gradually add dry ingredients to wet ingredients, mixing until a soft dough forms.
6. Roll dough into 1-inch balls and place 2 inches apart on baking sheets. Flatten slightly with your hand.
7. Bake for 10–12 minutes, until cookies are set. Cool on baking sheets for 5 minutes, then transfer to a wire rack.
8. For the glaze, whisk powdered sugar and lemon juice in a small bowl until smooth. Brush glaze over cooled cookies and let set for 10 minutes.

Almond Molasses Brittle

Total Time: 25 minutes + 1 hour cooling

This crunchy brittle with toasty molasses and anise snaps like a sweet find at a Weihnachtsmarkt stall.

- 1 cup granulated sugar
- ½ cup light corn syrup
- ¼ cup molasses
- 2 tbsp unsalted butter
- ½ tsp ground anise
- ¼ tsp salt
- 1 tsp baking soda
- 1 cup whole almonds, toasted

1. Line a baking sheet with parchment paper and lightly grease with butter.
2. In a medium saucepan, combine sugar, corn syrup, and molasses. Cook over medium heat, stirring occasionally, until mixture reaches 300°F on a candy thermometer (about 8–10 minutes).
3. Remove from heat and quickly stir in butter, ground anise, salt, and baking soda (mixture will foam).
4. Stir in almonds and immediately pour onto the prepared baking sheet, spreading into a thin layer with a spatula.
5. Let the brittle cool at room temperature for 1 hour, or until hardened.
6. Break into bite-sized pieces. Store in an airtight container.

17

Door 17

Chestnut Chocolate Chip Cookies

Total Time: 45 minutes

Chewy cookies with nutty chestnut puree and semi-sweet chocolate taste like roasting nuts by a crackling fire.

- 2 cups all-purpose flour
- ½ tsp baking powder
- ¼ tsp salt
- ¾ cup unsalted butter, softened
- ¾ cup granulated sugar
- 1 large egg
- 1 tsp vanilla extract
- ½ cup chestnut puree (canned or vacuum-packed)
- ¾ cup semi-sweet chocolate chips

1. Preheat oven to 350°F (175°C). Line two baking sheets with parchment paper.
2. In a medium bowl, whisk together flour, baking powder, and salt. Set aside.
3. In a large bowl, cream butter and sugar with an electric mixer until light and fluffy (about 2 minutes).
4. Add egg, vanilla extract, and chestnut puree, beating until combined.
5. Gradually add dry ingredients to wet ingredients, mixing until a soft dough forms. Fold in chocolate chips.
6. Roll dough into 1-inch balls and place 2 inches apart on baking sheets. Flatten slightly with your hand.
7. Bake for 10–12 minutes, until edges are set. Cool on baking sheets for 5 minutes, then transfer to a wire rack to cool completely.

Spiced Chocolate Hazelnut Fudge

Total Time: 15 minutes + 2 hours chilling

This creamy fudge with crunchy hazelnuts and silky dark chocolate feels like a nutty treat warmed by the fireside.

- 12 oz dark chocolate chips (60-70% cocoa)
- 14 oz sweetened condensed milk
- ½ cup hazelnuts, toasted and chopped
- 1 tsp ground cinnamon
- ½ tsp ground nutmeg
- ¼ tsp ground cloves
- 1 tsp vanilla extract
- Pinch of salt

1. Line an 8x8-inch baking pan with parchment paper. Set aside.
2. Melt dark chocolate chips and sweetened condensed milk in a saucepan over low heat. Stir constantly.
3. Remove from heat. Stir in cinnamon, nutmeg, cloves, vanilla extract, and salt.
4. Fold in chopped hazelnuts until evenly distributed.
5. Pour mixture into the prepared pan. Spread evenly with a spatula.
6. Chill in the refrigerator for 2-3 hours until firm.
7. Cut into squares and serve as a festive holiday treat.

18

Door 18

White Chocolate Cranberry Cookies

Total Time: 35 minutes

Soft, buttery cookies with chewy cranberries, white chocolate, and a hint of orange blossom taste like picking roses in a snowy winter garden.

2 ¼ cups all-purpose flour
1 cup unsalted butter, softened
¾ cup granulated sugar
½ cup brown sugar
1 large egg
1 tsp vanilla extract
1 tsp orange blossom water
½ tsp baking soda
½ tsp salt
¾ cup dried cranberries
¾ cup white chocolate chips

1. Preheat oven to 350°F. Line a baking sheet with parchment paper.
2. Cream butter, granulated sugar, and brown sugar in a bowl until light and fluffy.
3. Add egg, vanilla extract, and orange blossom water. Mix well.
4. Whisk flour, baking soda, and salt in another bowl. Gradually add to the butter mixture.
5. Fold in dried cranberries and white chocolate chips.
6. Drop tablespoon-sized portions of dough onto the baking sheet. Space 2 inches apart.
7. Bake for 10-12 minutes until edges are lightly golden. Cool on the sheet for 5 minutes. Transfer to a rack.

Chocolate Cherry Truffles

Total Time: 20 minutes + 1 hour chilling

Velvety truffles with a sweet cherry center shine like blooming roses in a snowy garden.

- ½ cup heavy cream
- 12 oz semi-sweet chocolate chips, divided
- 2 tbsp unsalted butter
- 24 maraschino cherries, drained and patted dry
- 1 tsp vanilla extract
- Pinch of salt
- 2 oz semi-sweet chocolate chips (for drizzling)

1. Heat heavy cream in a saucepan over medium heat until it begins to simmer.
2. Pour hot cream over 12 oz semi-sweet chocolate chips in a bowl. Let sit for 2 minutes.
3. Stir until chocolate is fully melted and smooth. Add butter, vanilla extract, and salt.
4. Chill mixture in the refrigerator for 1-2 hours until firm but workable.
5. Scoop a tablespoon of chocolate mixture. Flatten it and place a maraschino cherry in the center. Roll into a ball around the cherry.
6. Melt 2 oz semi-sweet chocolate chips in a microwave-safe bowl. Heat in 20-second intervals.
7. Drizzle melted chocolate over each truffle. Let set at room temperature or chill for 15 minutes. Serve.

Door 19

Vanilla Cream Cheese Cookies

Total Time: 45 minutes

Soft, vanilla-rich cookies with a tangy cream cheese bite feel like snowflakes melting on your tongue.

- 2½ cups all-purpose flour
- ½ tsp baking powder
- ¼ tsp salt
- ½ cup unsalted butter, softened
- 4 oz cream cheese, softened
- ¾ cup granulated sugar
- 1 large egg
- 2 tsp vanilla extract
- ¼ cup powdered sugar (for dusting)

1. Preheat oven to 350°F (175°C). Line two baking sheets with parchment paper.
2. In a medium bowl, whisk together flour, baking powder, and salt. Set aside.
3. In a large bowl, cream butter, cream cheese, and granulated sugar with an electric mixer until light and fluffy (about 2 minutes).
4. Add egg and vanilla extract, beating until combined.
5. Gradually add dry ingredients to wet ingredients, mixing until a soft dough forms.
6. Roll dough into 1-inch balls and place 2 inches apart on baking sheets.
7. Bake for 10–12 minutes, until edges are set but cookies remain pale. Cool on baking sheets for 5 minutes, then transfer to a wire rack.
8. Dust cooled cookies with powdered sugar for a snowy effect.

Peanut Butter Cream Cheese Fudge

Total Time: 15 minutes + 2 hours chilling

Smooth peanut butter fudge with vanilla and tangy cream cheese melts in your mouth like falling snowflakes.

8 oz cream cheese, softened
1 cup creamy peanut butter
½ cup unsalted butter
1 tsp vanilla extract
2 cups powdered sugar
Pinch of salt

1. Line an 8x8-inch baking pan with parchment paper. Set aside.
2. Beat cream cheese, peanut butter, and butter in a large bowl until smooth.
3. Add vanilla extract and salt. Mix well.

   Gradually add powdered sugar. Beat until the mixture is thick and creamy.
4. Spread the mixture evenly into the prepared pan.
5. Chill in the refrigerator for 2-3 hours until firm. Cut into squares and serve.

Door 20

Lemon Poppy Seed Cookies

Total Time: 50 minutes

Crispy cookies with crunchy poppy seeds, zesty lemon, and honey taste like a cozy Christmas Eve treat.

- 2 cups all-purpose flour
- ½ tsp baking powder
- ½ tbsp lemon zest
- ¼ tsp salt
- ¾ cup unsalted butter, softened
- ¾ cup granulated sugar
- 1 large egg
- 1 tsp vanilla extract
- 2 tbsp honey
- ¼ cup poppy seeds

1. Preheat oven to 350°F (175°C). Line two baking sheets with parchment paper.
2. In a medium bowl, whisk together flour, baking powder, lemon zest, and salt. Set aside.
3. In a large bowl, cream butter and sugar with an electric mixer until light and fluffy (about 2 minutes).
4. Add egg, vanilla extract, honey, and poppy seeds, beating until combined.
5. Gradually add dry ingredients to wet ingredients, mixing until a soft dough forms.
6. Roll dough into 1-inch balls and place 2 inches apart on baking sheets. Flatten slightly with your hand.
7. Bake for 10–12 minutes, until edges are lightly golden. Cool on baking sheets for 5 minutes, then transfer to a wire rack to cool completely.

Spiced Peanut Brittle

Total Time: 15 minutes + 1 hour chilling

This sweet brittle with warm spices and peanuts crunches like a treat from a Wigilia celebration.

- 1 cup granulated sugar
- ½ cup light corn syrup
- ¼ cup water
- 1 cup unsalted peanuts
- 1 tsp ground cinnamon
- ½ tsp ground nutmeg
- ¼ tsp ground cloves
- 1 tsp vanilla extract
- 1 tsp baking soda
- 2 tbsp unsalted butter

1. Line a baking sheet with parchment paper. Set aside.
2. Combine sugar, corn syrup, and water in a medium saucepan over medium heat.
3. Stir until sugar dissolves. Cook until mixture reaches 250°F on a candy thermometer.
4. Add peanuts, cinnamon, nutmeg, and cloves. Stir constantly until mixture reaches 300°F.
5. Remove from heat. Stir in vanilla extract, baking soda, and butter until foamy.
6. Pour onto the prepared baking sheet. Spread quickly with a spatula.
7. Let cool completely for 1-2 hours. Break into pieces and serve.

Door 21

Orange Slice Cookies

Total Time: 35 minutes

Buttery cookies with crisp bottoms and a candied orange slice on top warm you like a cozy seat by the hearth.

- ½ cup unsalted butter, softened
- ¾ cup granulated sugar
- 1 large egg
- 1 tsp vanilla extract
- 1 ½ cups all-purpose flour
- ½ tsp baking powder
- ¼ tsp salt
- 1 medium orange, thinly sliced (about 12 slices)
- ½ cup water
- ½ cup sugar (for candying orange slices)
- 1 tbsp orange zest

1. Preheat oven to 350°F. Line a baking sheet with parchment paper.
2. Cream butter and ¾ cup sugar in a bowl until light and fluffy. Add egg, vanilla extract, and orange zest.
3. Whisk flour, baking powder, and salt in another bowl. Gradually mix into the butter mixture.
4. Drop tablespoon-sized portions of dough onto the baking sheet. Space 2 inches apart.
5. Combine ½ cup water and ½ cup sugar in a small saucepan. Bring to a boil.
6. Add orange slices. Simmer for 10 minutes until translucent. Drain and place one slice on each dough ball.
7. Bake for 10-12 minutes until edges are lightly golden. Cool on the sheet for 5 minutes. Transfer to a rack.

Candied Orange Slices

Total Time: 2 hours + 15 minutes chilling

These crisp orange slices are coated in silky dark chocolate for a treat that feels like a sweet spark from the hearth.

- 2 cups water
- 2 cups granulated sugar
- 2 large oranges, thinly sliced
- 8 oz dark chocolate chips (60-70% cocoa)
- 1 tsp coconut oil (optional, for smoother chocolate)
- Pinch of salt

1. Combine water and sugar in a large saucepan. Bring to a boil over medium heat.
2. Add orange slices. Simmer for 45-60 minutes until translucent and syrup thickens.
3. Remove slices with a slotted spoon. Lay flat on a wire rack to dry for 1-2 hours.
4. Melt dark chocolate chips with coconut oil in a microwave-safe bowl. Heat in 20-second intervals.
5. Dip half of each orange slice into the melted chocolate. Let excess drip off.
6. Place slices on a parchment-lined baking sheet. Sprinkle with a pinch of salt.
7. Chill in the refrigerator for 15-20 minutes until chocolate sets. Serve.

Door 22

White Chocolate Chip Almond Cookies

Total Time: 30 minutes

Buttery almond cookies with crunchy macadamias and white chocolate chips shine like snowflakes catching starlight.

- 2 cups all-purpose flour
- ¾ cup almond flour
- ½ tsp baking powder
- ¼ tsp salt
- ¾ cup unsalted butter, softened
- ¾ cup granulated sugar
- 1 large egg
- 1 large egg yolk
- 1 tsp almond extract
- ½ tsp vanilla extract
- ½ cup white chocolate chips
- ½ cup chopped macadamias

1. Preheat oven to 350°F. Line two baking sheets with parchment paper.
2. Whisk together flour, almond flour, baking powder, and salt in a medium bowl. Set aside.
3. Cream butter and sugar in a large bowl with an electric mixer until light and fluffy.
4. Add egg, egg yolk, almond extract, and vanilla extract. Beat until combined.
5. Gradually mix in dry ingredients. Fold in white chocolate chips and macadamias.
6. Drop tablespoon-sized portions of dough onto baking sheets.
7. Bake for 8-10 minutes until edges are lightly golden. Cool on baking sheets for 5 minutes. Transfer to a rack.

White Chocolate Pomegranate Bark

Total Time: 15 minutes + 1 hour chilling

Crunchy white chocolate bark with nutty almonds and tart pomegranate seeds sparkles like snow under a starry sky.

- 16 oz white chocolate chips
- 1 tsp coconut oil (optional, for smoother melting)
- ¾ cup almonds, toasted and chopped
- ½ cup pomegranate seeds
- Pinch of salt

1. Line a baking sheet with parchment paper. Set aside.
2. Melt white chocolate chips with coconut oil in a microwave-safe bowl. Heat in 20-second intervals.
3. Stir until smooth. Add a pinch of salt.
4. Spread melted chocolate evenly onto the prepared baking sheet into a thin layer.
5. Sprinkle chopped almonds and pomegranate seeds over the chocolate.
6. Chill in the refrigerator for 1-2 hours until fully set.
7. Break into pieces and serve as a festive holiday treat.

23

Door 23

Cinnamon Apple Oatmeal Cookies

Total Time: 35 minutes

Chewy oatmeal cookies with sweet apples and earthy cinnamon smell like Christmas Eve's warm, magical glow.

- 1 ½ cups old-fashioned oats
- 1 cup all-purpose flour
- ½ tsp baking soda
- ½ tsp ground cinnamon
- ¼ tsp salt
- ½ cup unsalted butter, softened
- ¾ cup brown sugar
- 1 large egg
- 1 tsp vanilla extract
- 1 cup fresh apple, peeled and finely chopped (about 1 medium apple)
- ¼ tsp ground nutmeg

1. Preheat oven to 350°F. Line a baking sheet with parchment paper.
2. Whisk oats, flour, baking soda, cinnamon, nutmeg, and salt in a medium bowl. Set aside.
3. Cream butter and brown sugar in a large bowl until light and fluffy.
4. Add egg and vanilla extract. Beat until combined.
5. Gradually mix in dry ingredients. Fold in chopped apple.
6. Drop tablespoon-sized portions of dough onto the baking sheet. Space 2 inches apart.
7. Bake for 10-12 minutes until edges are golden. Cool on the sheet for 5 minutes. Transfer to a rack.

Raspberry Cream Cheese Truffles

Total Time: 20 minutes + 1 hour chilling

These cream cheese-white chocolate truffles rolled in tart raspberry powder taste like the sweet magic of Christmas Eve night.

- 8 oz white chocolate chips
- 8 oz cream cheese, softened
- ¼ cup powdered sugar
- 1 tsp vanilla extract
- Pinch of salt
- ½ cup freeze-dried raspberries (ground into powder)
- 1 tbsp unsalted butter

1. Melt white chocolate chips and butter in a microwave-safe bowl. Heat in 20-second intervals.
2. Stir until smooth. Let cool slightly.
3. Beat cream cheese, powdered sugar, vanilla extract, and salt in a bowl until creamy.
4. Mix melted chocolate into the cream cheese mixture until well combined.
5. Chill in the refrigerator for 1-2 hours until firm enough to shape.
6. Scoop tablespoon-sized portions. Roll into balls and then coat in freeze-dried raspberry powder.
7. Store in an airtight container in the fridge. Serve chilled.

24

Door 24

Double Chocolate Hazelnut Cookies

Total Time: 50 minutes

These chocolate cookies with crunchy hazelnuts and rich dark chocolate burst with joy for a perfect Christmas morning.

- 2 ¼ cups all-purpose flour
- ¼ cup unsweetened cocoa powder
- 1 tsp baking soda
- ¼ tsp salt
- ¾ cup unsalted butter, softened
- ¾ cup light brown sugar, packed
- ½ cup granulated sugar
- 1 large egg
- 1 tsp vanilla extract
- ¾ cup chopped hazelnuts
- ½ cup dark chocolate chips

1. Preheat oven to 350°F (175°C). Line two baking sheets with parchment paper.
2. In a medium bowl, whisk together flour, cocoa powder, baking soda, and salt. Set aside.
3. In a large bowl, cream butter, brown sugar, and granulated sugar with an electric mixer until light and fluffy (about 2 minutes).
4. Add egg and vanilla extract, beating until combined.
5. Gradually add dry ingredients to wet ingredients, mixing until a soft dough forms. Fold in chopped hazelnuts and chocolate chips.
6. Roll dough into 1-inch balls and place 2 inches apart on baking sheets. Flatten slightly with your hand.
7. Bake for 10–12 minutes, until edges are set. Cool on baking sheets for 5 minutes, then transfer to a wire rack to cool completely.

Hazelnut Sea Salt Chocolate Fudge

Total Time: 25 minutes + 2 hours chilling

Silky chocolate fudge with chopped hazelnuts and coarse sea salt crunches with festive delight to start Christmas Day.

- 14 oz sweetened condensed milk
- 1 ½ cups semi-sweet chocolate chips
- 1 cup chocolate hazelnut spread (e.g., Nutella)
- ½ cup chopped hazelnuts
- 1 tsp vanilla extract
- ¼ tsp salt
- ½ tsp coarse sea salt (for topping)

1. Line an 8x8-inch baking dish with parchment paper. Leave overhang for easy removal.
2. Combine sweetened condensed milk, chocolate chips, and chocolate hazelnut spread in a medium saucepan over low heat.
3. Stir constantly until melted and smooth. This takes about 5-7 minutes.
4. Remove from heat. Stir in vanilla extract, salt, and chopped hazelnuts.
5. Pour the mixture into the prepared dish. Smooth the top with a spatula.
6. Sprinkle coarse sea salt evenly over the top.
7. Refrigerate for 2 hours until firm. Lift fudge from the dish using the parchment overhang. Cut into 1-inch squares. Store in an airtight container in the fridge.

Printed in Dunstable, United Kingdom

71538008R00057